House Beautiful

500 SENSATIONAL WAYS TO CREATE YOUR IDEAL HOME

From the Editors of *House Beautiful*

HEARST BOOKS

A division of Sterling Publishing Co., Inc.

New York / London

www.sterlingpublishing.com

Library of Congress Cataloging-in-Publication Data

Sloan, Kate.
House beautiful: 500 sensational ways to create your ideal home / Kate Sloan.
p. cm.
Includes index.
ISBN-13: 978-1-58816-604-3
ISBN-10: 1-58816-604-X
1. Interior decoration--Handbooks, manuals, etc. I. House beautiful.. II. Title. III. Title: 500 sensational ways to create your ideal home.
NK2115.N33 2007
747--dc22
2006027592

10 9 8 7 6 5 4 3 2
Second edition November 2007
Published by Hearst Books
A Division of Sterling Publishing Co., Inc.
387 Park Avenue South, New York, NY 10016

www.housebeautiful.com

Cover and interior design by 3+Co. (www.threeandco.com)
Jacket photographs: *front cover*, Ken Hayden; *spine*, Hugh Stewart; *back cover right*, John M. Hall; *back cover left*, Eric Piasecki

For information about custom editions, special sales, premium and corporate purchases, please contact
Sterling Special Sales Department at 800-805-5489 or specialsales@sterlingpub.com.

Distributed in Canada by Sterling Publishing
c/o Canadian Manda Group, 165 Dufferin Street
Toronto, Ontario, Canada M6K 3H6

Distributed in Australia by Capricorn Link (Australia) Pty. Ltd.
P.O. Box 704, Windsor, NSW 2756 Australia

Manufactured in China

ISBN 13: 978-1-58816-604-3
ISBN 10: 1-58816-604-X

House Beautiful

500 SENSATIONAL WAYS TO CREATE YOUR IDEAL HOME

Table of Contents

Introduction

CREATING AN IDEAL HOME is like venturing on a long journey. Even if it's carefully planned, the process is usually full of surprises. The best homes evolve over time. A good house or apartment should do more than provide shelter and creature comforts. It should also enhance your daily routine, brighten your spirits, stimulate your imagination, and ignite your passions. In short, the perfect home should reflect both who you are and who you want to become.

Designing a home, like living a life, is most fulfilling when it involves a sense of discovery. It should be embraced as a pleasurable work in progress. This endeavor is not so much about finding or defining your style as it is about surrounding yourself with the furnishings, colors, accents, and art that bring you pleasure. It's about knowing your likes and dislikes, then creating an environment that reinforces what you value and how you want to live. When you cultivate spaces that support your core needs and ideals, you won't wind up with cookie-cutter rooms or spaces that look like those of your next-door neighbor. Nor will your decor be driven by tradition or trends. Instead, your home will be an extension of your personality and your dreams.

Naturally, as each of us is unique, so are our dreams. Nonetheless, in order to develop an ideal home, it's helpful to home in on the essence of our dreams, which often reflect a mix of our past experience along with a vision of the future we want to create. Each chapter of this book represents one of seven different lifestyle ideals—or dreams. They were developed with an emphasis on personality types and inner needs, rather than style, to help you clarify what is most important to you as you cultivate the highest quality of life you can achieve.

Of course, quality of life will mean different things to different people. You might collect old master paintings, while your colleague collects contemporary photographs. Your childless neighbors might travel regularly to remote places all over the world, while your new-parent cousins prefer to keep family

doings contained in their own backyard. Some of us prefer to retreat to our own inner sanctums; some long to commune with nature. There are those for whom nothing but luxury will do, and there are those who feel that simple pleasures are the best.

On the pages that follow, you'll find rooms and gardens that will appeal to every personality type, plus a multitude of tips that can help you create your own ideal spaces. The rooms in one chapter may resonate with you immediately, while spaces in another might appeal to your spouse. More likely you'll see spaces and ideas in two or three chapters that support complementary or even conflicting dreams. The key is to look for the dominant themes that tempt you and balance the preferences of everyone who shares your home.

It's also crucial to consider your context and accept its limitations while nurturing its possibilities. You can no sooner turn a quarter of an acre into a nature preserve than you can transform a modern glass house into a country cottage.

Most of all, it's worthwhile to remember that creating the home of your dreams is not so much a goal as it is a process. This will make it easier for you to refresh and renew your house now and then—even if the essential impulse that inspired it remains the same. If you think of your home as a living organism, you'll adapt and change it patiently—both aesthetically and technologically—with an eye toward the big picture.

Before moving forward, we invite you to take the following quiz to see which personality type or dreamer emerges. Then turn to the chapter or chapters whose spaces most closely align with your dominant personality type—and let your dreams begin.

Quiz

Take this quick personality quiz to identify your design sensibility so that you can get started on creating the home of your dreams.

1. What would be an ideal vacation for you?

   A. A tour of some of the stately manors and gardens of England
   B. A safari in Africa or India
   C. A yoga/spa retreat in Costa Rica
   D. A week at your own summer house
   E. A nature trek in the Amazon or the Grand Canyon
   F. A week in a villa in Bali
   G. A trip to Nantucket or the Sonoma County wine country

2. Which type of clothing appeals to you most?

   A. A couture dress or a custom-made suit
   B. An Asian blouse or a vintage shirt paired with a designer skirt or trousers
   C. A chic linen dress in a neutral color or a comfortable cotton sweater and pants
   D. Khaki pants and button-down blouse or shirt
   E. Jeans and a T-shirt
   F. Something from Prada, Marc Jacobs, or Ann Demeulemeester
   G. A V-neck sweater and a classic skirt or pants

3. How would you most enjoy spending a free evening?

    A. At the opera, followed by dinner at a romantic French bistro

    B. Listening to a Cuban big band, followed by dinner at a Mediterranean restaurant

    C. Listening to a lecture on Tibetan spirituality, followed by dinner at a quiet sushi place or whole foods restaurant

    D. Staying at home with family or friends, ordering in, and watching a ball game or movie on television

    E. Dinner and drinks on an open-air terrace at a waterside restaurant, preferably one that serves organic food

    F. Attending an art opening, followed by dinner and drinks with friends at the latest hotspot in town

    G. Dinner with family at the local steak-and-lobster restaurant after an afternoon game of volleyball or croquet

4. If you had an hour or two to yourself how would you be most likely to spend your time?

    A. Attending a wine-and-cheese tasting event

    B. Visiting an Asian antiques shop

    C. Taking a yoga class or getting a massage

    D. Watching television

    E. Going for a hike in the mountains or walking along the beach

    F. Shopping at a designer boutique or high-end electronics store

    G. Reading the newspaper or a good book

5. Which of the following furnishings or accents appeals to you most?

    A. A French Regency desk

    B. A Moroccan side table

    C. A comfortable chair upholstered in neutral-colored linen

    D. An old trunk that could double as a coffee table

    E. A sisal or jute rug

    F. A mid-20th-century Italian chandelier

    G. A round pedestal dining table and Windsor chairs

6. Which of the following structures appeals to you most?

   A. A French château
   B. An Italian farmhouse
   C. A Japanese teahouse
   D. A cottage
   E. A beach house
   F. A contemporary home
   G. An English country house

7. If you had $5,000 to spend on anything for your home, what would it be?

   A. Some very fine wine and a sterling silver champagne bucket
   B. An Asian carpet
   C. A landscape painting or a soothing work of abstract art
   D. Some new kitchen appliances or built-in cabinets
   E. An outdoor fireplace, grill, or patio furniture
   F. A flat-screen television
   G. New bed linens, possibly an antique side table or an addition to a collection of transferware, plus a few household repairs or upgrades, such as painting the walls or power-washing the deck

What your answers say about your design style

 If three or more of your answers were **A**s, you are likely to be most content in **Sophisticated Surroundings**.

 If three or more of your answers were **D**s, chances are you'll want to live in a **Comfortable Haven**.

 If three or more of your answers were **G**s, the ideal house for you is likely to be a **Welcoming Home**.

 If three or more of your answers were **B**s, you will probably feel most at ease in an **Eclectic Environment**.

 If three or more of your answers were **E**s, you're likely to seek out a **Natural Abode**.

If your answers indicate that you are drawn to two or more different styles, you can certainly combine the two looks to suit your tastes, or pick one of the styles and go with it.

 If three or more of your answers were **C**s, you will probably be drawn to a **Serene Retreat**.

 If three or more of your answers were **F**s, the best home for you is probably a **Bold Domain**.

Chapter 1 Sophisticated Surroundings

SOPHISTICATED SURROUNDINGS are for those who cherish the finest things in life. They are likely to be found in a formal home, inspired by stately English manors, sophisticated French châteaus, or elegant Italian palazzi. Their structure and form may be rooted firmly in the past, yet with interiors that are likely to include a refreshing mix of European or American antiques and fine art along with contemporary colors, creature comforts, and amenities. Public rooms are distinctly defined for specific purposes—formal and casual dining, reading, entertaining—while private rooms are the embodiment of luxury. Manicured gardens and grounds might include clipped parterres, a pergola or gazebo, and perhaps a garden folly, such as wedding-cake topiary.

Living Spaces

1

•

Place a skirted round table in one part of a large living room and surround it with upholstered benches to define a distinct seating zone for reading or taking tea.

2

•

Refresh a traditional room that has a grand scale by keenly editing furnishings and restricting patterns to pillows and other decorative accents.

3

•

Cover the walls of a living room with custom-designed, hand-painted silk wallpaper and let it set the color scheme for the room.

4

Hang an unframed painting
in an entrance hall to fill a
large empty wall and provide
an elegant greeting for guests.

5

•

Bring a seasonal note to a cheerful window seat on a stair landing by filling a tall vase with flowering branches.

6
.

Allow antique furnishings and accents to stand out by limiting the palette of fabrics to creams and whites and setting them off with surfaces of stone and wood.

7
.

Hang a large painting above a staircase to create high visual impact.

8
•

Hang a Japanese screen over a Regency settee in an entrance hall to create a warm, rich, and striking effect.

9

●

Keep an expansive living
room vibrant by mixing styles
of furniture and collectibles,
all in the same color palette to
maintain a sense of unity.

10

•

Have the floor of an entry hall hand-painted with faux marquetry that matches the style of not only the hall but also the adjoining living room.

11

•

Shake up a Louis XVI canapé with bold stripes and leopard pillows that add a playful sophistication to the traditional antique.

12

Update the dark vestibule of an urban maisonette with a minimalist contemporary painting mounted above an intricately carved console.

13

•

Enrich a Louis XV settee with a trim in a contrasting color. Complement the richness of the ceiling-to-floor drapes with patterned cushions on the sofa.

14

•

Cover the floor with a wool carpet woven on an old loom in a subtle custom pattern. Choose a neutral color for versatility.

15

•

Use contrasting wall treatments in adjoining rooms. Shown here is a foyer with Chinese-themed wallpaper, while the living room displays antique British and American portraits.

16

•

Apply a custom glaze to the walls and mount a Regency-style mirror above an elegant mantel.

17

Cover the living room floor with a highly-patterned carpet and pick up its color palette in the walls, drapes, and furniture.

18

●

Restore the entrance of an old house to its former glory with period details and artisanal touches like handcrafted woodwork and antique tapestry.

19

Install a pair of chandeliers
to reflect antique silver-and-
gold tea-chest paper on
the cathedral ceiling of a
tall entrance hall.

20

Embellish a coffered
ceiling with delicate stencil
work and employ a densely
fringed, oversized ottoman
as a coffee table.

21

•

Pep up and modernize
a collection of traditional
living room furnishings with
leopard-print accents.

22

•

Top the mantel in a drawing
room with an ornate mirror
(here, in the 18th-century
Irish Gothic style) and
cover the walls with a
complementary wallpaper.

Dining Rooms
& Breakfast Nooks

23

●

Display and protect a
collection of antique
blue-and-white porcelain
in a corner hutch in
the dining room of a
weekend house.

24

•

Cover the walls with
hand-painted wallpaper
that echoes the floral
patterns and color palettes
of antique ceramic jars.

25

●

Instead of using wallpaper, cover the walls of a dining room with a large collection of antique prints.

26

●

Place an arrangement of *Lysimachia ciliata* 'Purpurea,' magnolia seed pods, and skimmia berries in a silver footed urn on a sideboard.

27

•

Place a distinctive item of
interest in the room—
here a French terra-cotta
wall fountain complemented
by Regency-style chairs
upholstered in a bold pattern.

28

•

Bring a formal touch to a
dining table in a country
house by topping it with a
pristine vintage tablecloth
and setting it with fine china.

29

•

Enliven a dining room table with a pair of Chippendale-style chairs and cover the others in a mix of onyx leather and damask in a vivid hue.

30

•

Add an elegant note to a breakfast nook in a country house by slipcovering chairs in toile fabric and adding crisp trim at the edge of the skirts.

31

•

Commission a mural for the walls and include a round Regency mahogany table and chairs with quatrefoil backs and turquoise leather seat cushions.

32

•

Treat the walls of a formal dining room to multiple coats of brown lacquer for a rich and lustrous effect.

33

Instead of one long
rectangular table, choose
two smaller round tables to
give a formal dining room
a fresh twist that promotes
intimate conversations.

34

•

Cover the walls of a dining room with a floral wallpaper and fill a large urn with flowering branches that echo the theme.

35

For a black-tie New Year's Eve dinner, tuck a monogram into tiny silver-plate frames for guests at each place setting.

36

Follow the 19th-century custom of including a smaller, skirted luncheon table in the same room as the main dining table.

Kitchens & Pantries

37
●

Have a custom hood installed over a large, professional cooking suite topped with stainless steel counters.

38
●

Create a dramatic focal point in a kitchen by integrating a Tuscan-inspired hearth and placing a pair of white loggia chairs in front of it.

39

Add color and texture to a light, monochromatic kitchen with an interesting flooring—such as the red and beige checked floors here.

40

Build a butler's pantry with a swinging door next to the kitchen and enhance the cabinet doors with handsome bullet hinges. Here, the counters are topped with Calacatta Gold marble.

41

•

Fill a tall pot with
ease right on the stove
by installing an adjustable
pivoting faucet behind
the cooktop.

Libraries, Dens & Offices

42

●

Fill the shelves of a library
with art books and display a
collection of prints with
identical matting and frames.

43

•

Place a plaster bust on a
heavily carved writing
table to create a classical
look echoed in an ornate
mirror over the mantle.

44

Set a warm, welcoming tone in a sitting room with a fabulous Chinese rug and modern wingback chairs flanking the fireplace.

45

Mount extendable brass lamps that hang over built-in bookshelves to aid in finding books in the evenings.

46

•

Hang engravings (here a series of 17th- and 18th-century Dutch works) above a fireplace to add an historical element to a music room or study.

47

•

Include a pair of antique Regency chairs in a library and brighten the windows with Roman shades made with a lively fabric that still lets light through.

48

•

Give a library with Tudoresque windows a theatrical quality using intensely colored walls and draperies trimmed with extra-long fringe.

49

•

The angle of the sun changes the nature of color—such as a deep red on the walls—so be sure to take location into account when choosing a color scheme.

50

•

Add zest to a library by upholstering furniture in bright red-and-white crewel fabric and covering the floor with an ocelot-patterned carpet.

51

●

An ornate feature—such as this 17th-century Baroque fireplace—requires bold companions, such as a dramatic rug and boldly detailing ceiling.

52

●

Choose a palette for a room starting with a painting or carpet you plan to use in it.

53

●

For a heady glamour in a
living room, include a mix
of treasures like a screen,
a large piece of branching
coral, a zebra-skin rug,
and a chaise longue.

54

•

Mount a freewheeling yet
symmetrical arrangement
of pictures above an
overstuffed sofa covered
in chintz and topped
with plenty of pillows.

55

•

Separate public from
private rooms with a padded
door covered with baize
and monogrammed with
French nails.

56

●

Maximize the height and
elegance of a dressing room
by lining both sides of
the space with carefully
proportioned wardrobes.

57

Mount an embroidered hanging from India on the wall behind a mirrored four-poster bed, and complement the hanging with a large rug in the same color palette.

58

•

Top a bed with a sumptuous canopy that features the same design as the wallpaper, upholstered headboard, pillow shams, and even an eye mask.

59

●

Enrich the walls of a master
suite with a pattern of subtle
stripes. Echo the wall color
in the upholstered headboard
and canopy fabric.

60

Give a luxurious guest room French country charm with downy toile bed linens and an upholstered headboard.

61

Top the barley-twist bedposts of an ebonized bed with a blue velvet bed valence trimmed with gold braid and curtains that can be pulled open and closed.

62

Enrich a vaulted ceiling of the sitting area of a master bedroom with hand-painted scenery and an elegantly understated chandelier.

63

Add style and function to a little girl's room with built-in clothing armoires whose windows are lined with pale pink fabric panels.

64

•

Use one pattern in a small boy's room for the wallpaper, upholstered headboard, bed skirt, and draperies. Top the bed with simple linens to provide a visual break from the pattern.

65

•

Place a seat, here a gilded-and-lacquered Hepplewhite bench, at the foot of a canopied four-poster bed in a room where pink is anything but frivolous.

66

Give character to a guest
room with draperies and bed
hangings made from antique
toile that complements a
delightful hand-painted
antique chest used as a
side table.

Bathrooms

67
•

Position a linen-velvet upholstered wing chair next to an antique-style tub to bring a sense of comfort to an expansive bathroom.

68
•

Install caramel-colored onyx on the floor, counters, tub deck, and shower walls of a master bath.

69

Create an air of 1930s glamour in a bathroom with mirrored walls and doors and a sumptuous vintage-style tub.

70

Feel free, in an oversize bathroom to place an ornate side chair, antique plant stand, and Oriental rug.

Outdoor Rooms & Sunrooms

71

Include potted orange trees or aspidistra plants to add greenery to a long, narrow colonnaded second-floor gallery.

72

•

Top a *faux bois* table on a porch with a candelabrum and handblown wine glasses for a late-summer brunch.

73

•

Frame a view into a sunroom with a fresh-hued tartan fabric portiere and cover the windows with lace shades.

74

•

Complement floral patterns in a sunroom with fresh flowers and flowering plants.

Gardens

75

•

In a private garden surrounded
by a tall brick wall, create an
Edenesque lawn with ribbons
of box-framed parterres.

76

•

Give a large expanse of
lawn a more pleasing scale
and proportion by defining
it with beds in a pattern
along the sides.

77

Install a stone fountain as an elegant focal point in the center of a formal garden surrounded by mature trees.

78

●

Add texture to an elaborate garden with a stone wall assembled in a way that makes it look natural to its surroundings.

79

●

Curve garden edges along or around the lawn for a more organic, less cultivated look.

80

•

In the realm of fantasy: If you've got acres and acres and love wine, grow your own grapes.

81

•

Separate a terrace from the lawn with a semicircular bed surrounding a small pool and fountain, and add color to the house with climbing bougainvillea.

82

•

Make use of a hillside by
turning it into a multilevel
garden with sharply angled
and curved plants and
stepping stones.

83

•

Soften the geometry of the clipped hedges and obelisks of a formal French-style garden with flowers in a limited palette, such as white cosmos, purple salvia, and yellow rudbeckia.

84

•

Enrich a formal garden with a luminescent quality at dusk by planting white flowering plants and trees, such as 'Natchez' crepe myrtle, camellias, oak-leaf hydrangeas, magnolias, impatiens, azaleas, Mexican plum, and caladiums.

85

•

Encircle a painted terra-cotta
urn with Asian jasmine in a
garden for a heavenly scent.

86

•

Plant creeping fig to cover
a brick wall enclosing a
formal garden and trim it
twice a week in summer.

Chapter 2 Eclectic Environment

· 102 ·

· 106 ·

· 112 ·

· 114 ·

· 118 ·

· 121 ·

· 126 ·

· 129 ·

· 133 ·

· 140 ·

· 142 ·

· 144 ·

· 147 ·

· 151 ·

· 156 ·

THE ECLECTIC ENVIRONMENT is home to the worldly adventurer. Artfully peppered with an exotic mix of furnishings and artifacts from faraway places, its living spaces may house a lantern from Morocco, a coffee table from India, and colorful silk cushions from Thailand. These spaces may just as soon include a commingling of modern art and antique furniture, or contemporary furniture and primitive accents from Africa or South America. Talismans from around the globe—a pre-Columbian figurine, perhaps, or a 19th-century Chinese Buddha—infuse private spaces with energy and individuality. Outside, a Chinese lantern might illuminate a Tahitian teak table surrounded by Portuguese chairs.

The only constant in such homes is the element of surprise.

Living Spaces

87

•

Create a modern fusion look
in a sitting room with a mix
of Asian, contemporary,
and European furnishings in
a monochromatic palette.

88

For an unusal display, mount a door—here an 18th-century carved wooden one from the Piedmont region of Italy—on the wall of a high-ceilinged living room.

89

Evoke a masculine atmosphere in a drawing room by mixing hand-wrought elements from different places and periods, such as a rusted metal chandelier, an antique carved statue of a saint, and 18th-century armchairs.

90

•

Mix antiques, such as this William IV rosewood table, with modern art, such as this photograph by Valerie Belin, to give fresh energy to a living room.

91

•

Lacquer the walls of a room with white high-gloss paint to allow an array of multicultural furnishings from different eras to stand out in relief.

92

•

Enliven a traditional room paneled in mahogany by painting the ceiling with a geometric pattern and adding mid-20th-century furnishings from Italy, France, and America. The result: a timeless look.

93

•

Cover pillows on a sofa
with variegated Indian silks
that add pattern to a largely
patternless room.

94

•

Blend a mix of antique
furnishings from different
eras and places, such as this
19th-century Italian gilt
mirror, 18th-century
apothecary jars, and a 17th-
century English hall chair, to
add interest to a living room.

95

●

Set off contemporary
furniture with a mix of
antiques, mid-20th-
century pieces, a fanciful
crystal chandelier, and a
faux-skin rug.

96

Brighten a dark, moody entrance hall of a Tudor structure by gray-washing the architectural timbers, painting the floor with an appealing geometric pattern, and placing potted topiaries in rush baskets for a modern sensibility.

97

•

Enrich a great room with a mix
of periods and styles—here,
Louis XV chairs, a teak table
from Thailand, and a shepherd's
chest from Greece.

98

•

Cover the living room floor
with a dramatic rug and
dress the windows with
draperies made of a heavy
and striking fabric.

99

•

Refresh traditional pieces
with a surprising upholstery
fabric and trim treatment.

100

•

Create a little tension in a living room by mixing something modern, like a painting by Yayoi Kusama, with something baroque, such as an antique French chandelier.

101

•

Upholster a pair of formal chairs with raffia and white canvas, and place them on either side of a large armoire.

102

Install a creamy carpet with a nail-head trim in the anteroom of a living space and have the walls painted with a chinoiserie mural.

103

Give a family room energy with a worldly mix of furnishings, such as a pair of Brighton Pavilion–inspired tortoise-shell bamboo chairs, a polished dark-wood African stool, and some contemporary X benches covered in deer skin.

Dining Rooms & Breakfast Nooks

104

●

Bring a spicy note to a dining room by loosely hanging a boldly patterned antique Indian appliquéd textile on one wall.

105

●

Add an untraditional touch to a dining room by placing an unexpected lighting fixture—a floor lamp—next to the table.

106

•

Slipcover dining chairs with peppy Indian cotton stripes and hang a graphic white plaster-of-Paris candle chandelier over the middle of the table.

107

•

Hang a tapestry in a formal and
high-ceilinged dining room.

108

•

Separate the dining area of a
country guest house from the
sleeping area with rolling barn
doors. Add modern touches—
such as the industrial lighting
fixture over the table—to mix
up the styles.

109

Bring an unconventional touch to the dining area of a ranch house by upholstering chairs in pink-and-peach Fortuny fabric.

110

Juxtapose a dark carved refectory table with a modern pendant light fixture and an abstract painting.

111

Create a dining room table centerpiece from ostrich eggs and bone accessories.

112

•

Carve out a charming breakfast nook by placing a round table in front of an upholstered bench and pulling up a couple of mismatched stools.

113

•

Add texture to the wall of a small dining area with a trellis-like design behind an overstuffed banquette.

114

Add an unexpected modern element—such as this Lichtenstein print above the fireplace—to an otherwise traditional dining room.

Kitchens
& Pantries

115

●

Use antique tiles on the
floor and backsplash of a
rustic kitchen and surround
a central table with
contemporary chairs.

116

•

Commission an artisan to
craft a pair of freestanding
cabinets and have them painted
a lively color, such as golden
chartreuse, and then distressed
for an aged look.

117

•

Hand-paint the names of
French desserts on tin storage
bins stashed in the open shelves
of a kitchen island.

118

•

Add a touch of whimsy to a
kitchen by hanging a delicate
chandelier over an island.

119

Display a collection in an elegant wooden dresser. Here are French handblown antique bottles and contemporary salad plates in an 18th-century Alsatian hutch.

120

•

Mix modern elements, such
as Knoll bar stools or a classic
George Nelson pendant
with Arts and Crafts–style
cabinets in a kitchen.

Libraries, Dens & Offices

121

•

Furnish a study with an artful mélange of pieces, such as an Oriental rug, alabaster table lamps, Roman end tables, and a Swedish coffee table. (The one shown here is made from rosewood, zebrawood, and ebonized birch.)

122

●

Add interest and function
to a gallery leading to a
study by incorporating a
Chinese altar table for stacks
of books and collectibles.

123

●

Add color and shimmer to a Middle-Eastern–inspired reading nook with lots of colorful silk-covered pillows and silk-upholstered walls.

124

•

Give a reading room in a
ranch house an air of bohemian
luxury by covering the floor
with an Oriental rug and
placing assorted chinoiserie
pieces on shelves.

125

Cover one wall with an assemblage of offbeat works of art, including paintings, drawings, masks, and other collected items to give a home office unconventional flair.

126

•

Use unusual decorative textiles for window treatments. Here an antique *suzani* is used for a Roman shade.

127

•

Brighten up a study or den by painting built-in bookshelves a vibrant yellow or other cheerful color.

Bedrooms

128
●

Give a guest room personality
by making a gorgeous iron bed
the focal point. Shown here is
a 17th-century Tuscan bed.

129

•

Place a trunk or sailor's chest at the foot of a bed in a beachside vacation home. The one shown here comes from Greece and was hand-painted.

130

•

Place a provincial 18th-century Italian table on wheels between a pair of Colonial-style twin beds in a guest room.

131

•

Display a one-of-a-kind
collection—shown here are
carved *santos* and religious
artifacts—on a ledge above
the bed in a guest room.

132

Evoke a Russian dacha in the guest room of an American cabin with a canopied bed, an antler mirror, and a painted chest of drawers.

133

•

Add personality to a bedroom with a dramatic decoupaged chest topped with a simple mirror, small painting, elaborate lamp, and unique sculpture.

134

•

Display treasures from your travels. Shown here are an 18th-century Thai monk's bench used as a night table, and topped with a pair of Burmese teardrop mirrors and a contemporary lamp.

135

Cover a plain bed with a
dramatic bedspread or quilt
to add color and to make
up, visually, for the lack of
a headboard. Shown here
is an antique pink and
green *suzani*.

136

●

In a master bedroom, add
character by topping a
bench at the foot of the
bed with a kilim rug.

Bathrooms

137

•

Add character to a small
powder room by hanging a
custom-framed mirror
assembled from pieces of
antiqued mirror and rosettes.

138

●

Leave the door of a medicine cabinet open to display a visually interesting collection of glass bottles, canisters, and other toiletry containers.

139

●

Add drama and texture to a small bathroom by covering the walls with large, dark blue tiles.

140

Break from the usual and opt for tall matching lamps on a bathroom counter with two sinks, instead of mounted wall lighting.

141

Add a mirrored armoire in a large bathroom to ensure abundant storage space and provide the convenience of a full-length mirror.

142

•

Create an antique-country atmosphere in a bathroom by covering the top portion of the walls with wide horizonal natural-wood planks and the lower portion with white beadboard.

Outdoor Rooms & Sunrooms

143

●

Create a place for contemplation on a covered loggia by pairing a British Colonial chaise with an Asian stool, which can serve as a perch for a glass of wine and a book.

144

•

Add zest to a poolroom with a boldly striped wraparound sofa, red leather ottoman, and Moroccan-themed accents.

145

•

Add warmth to a sunroom by installing a fireplace and flanking it with a pair of painted rattan chaise longues that have thick cushions for extra comfort.

146

•

Add a playful note to an oceanfront gazebo by painting a Matisse-inspired frieze of frolicking swimmers near the ceiling.

Gardens

147

•

In keeping with the Creole tradition, paint the French doors of a *garçonnière* a bright coral color to lend punch to a courtyard and ensure a cheerful welcome upon arrival.

148

●

Bring an exotic look to a
labyrinth garden by installing a
Japanese-style bridge and planting
red Japanese maple trees.

149

●

Scatter columns of various
heights and styles throughout a
garden to get an eclectic look.

150

●

If your property is naturalistic and informal, consider adding a fieldstone-lined brook as a refreshing and casual water feature.

Chapter 3 Serene Retreat

THE SERENE RETREAT provides an oasis of comfort and calm for those who regard their home as a sanctuary. Imbued with quiet, neutral palettes, natural fabrics, and a minimalist mix of comfortable furnishings, the gathering spaces in these dwellings are as soothing to the senses as the private rooms. Subtle textures and patterns appeal to the eye; the sound of a trickling fountain provides a balm to frayed nerves; and candles, rosemary topiaries, or fresh flowers fill the air with a crisp, clean scent. The light from a single hurricane lamp might illuminate a covered terrace at night, or a Zenlike pool house might punctuate a view across a placid pool.

Living Spaces

151

Lighten up a traditional living room by adding new pieces with unfussy lines and white slipcovers or upholstery.

152

Install monochromatic floor-to-ceiling draperies to add softness to a formal living room.

153

●

Frame individual pieces of an antique map of a European city, such as Paris, and mount them on a wall in a living room to create an evocative yet tranquil backdrop.

154

As a foil for a serene room, include richly textured upholstery and unexpected touches, such as this modern lamp.

155

A high-backed sofa will lend intimacy to an expansive living room and makes a great spot for a nap as it envelopes you like a cocoon.

156

Place an extra-large leather
upholstered ottoman between
a pair of sofas and a couple of
chairs upholstered in muted
dusty hues of linen, such as
gray-blue or taupe.

157

Create a restful ambience in
a living room with fabrics and
furnishings in an easy-on-the-eye
palette of cream, beige, taupe, and
pale blue.

158

Paint the walls of a family room a soothing shade of pale green and keep fabric patterns subtle to cultivate relaxation and comfort.

159

Wash a living room in caramel, biscuit, and cream tones, and include subtly textured rugs to create a soothing atmosphere.

160

•

Bring out the drama of a grand, curving staircase in an entrance hall with stark walls and by paring furnishings and art to a minimum.

161

●

Objects don't have to be
placed symmetrically on a
mantel—a lone candlestick,
carved box, or interesting
vase can provide a perfect
finishing touch.

162

●

Hang a large, contemporary
black-and-white photograph
over a sofa in the living room
of a small urban apartment.

163

●

Set off sofas and chairs
covered in white cotton
duck with dark antique wood
furnishings in a high-ceilinged
living room.

164

●

Let the creams, browns, silvers, and grays of an antique Kirman rug inspire the palette for the furnishings, fabrics, and finishes in a living room.

165

●

Create an intimate gathering space by angling four wingback chairs around a starkly modern fireplace.

166

●

Carve out a private niche
in a family room by placing a
thickly cushioned window
seat—with a reading lamp
mounted on the wall—in a
remote corner.

Dining Rooms & Breakfast Nooks

167

•

Orient a long dining table toward oversized picture windows overlooking a view of a natural body of water or soothing landscape.

168

●

Inject a touch of sparkle
in a minimalist dining space
with a 1960s gold-plated
crystal chandelier.

169

●

Warm up an ultramodern
dining space with a macadamia-
colored calfskin floor covering
and some high-backed armchairs
upholstered in pale pistachio linen.

170

Create an all-white backdrop in a dining room and surround the table with comfortable leather chairs.

171

Top a banquette with a thick cushion and lots of silk pillows for extra seating in a dining room.

172

•

Set up a charming dining spot in a windowed corner of a kitchen with a pair of antique barstools and a tall bistro table.

173

•

Surround a round walnut table in a formal dining room with tufted chairs covered in plush mohair velvet.

174

•

Establish a soothing ambience
with furnishings and finishes in
a mix of materials, such as
a wrought-iron chandelier, a
table made of antique oak, and
bluestone flooring.

Kitchens & Pantries

175

•

Visually separate a kitchen
from an adjoining room or
a busy stairwell with a
Mondrianesque fiberglass
screen that shields the view
but still admits light.

176

Paint cabinetry in a country kitchen with stainless-steel appliances a restful, neutral color.

177

Forego window treatments in a kitchen to let in natural light and paint the walls varying shades of the subtlest greens.

178

Establish a sense of ease
and order in the kitchen by
positioning a pull-out pantry
next to the refrigerator.

179

Install a small sink in a
marble-topped kitchen
island for convenience while
prepping food.

180

•

Incorporate a wine
refrigerator and microwave
into the cabinetry so that
they blend into the style and
decor of the kitchen.

181

•

Create a sense of balance and harmony in a kitchen by contrasting white or cream-colored cabinetry with dark-wood barstools, cocoa-colored window shades, or a customized copper range hood.

Libraries, Dens & Offices

182

•

Hide books in a library on shelves behind paneled doors, where they will still be easily accessible.

183

•

Juxtapose pieces of different periods but with the same level of detail to project a balanced yet eclectic style.

184

Upholster a pair of wing chairs in a den with a subtle tweed in an oatmeal color.

185

Top a mantel with a striking bronze bust or contemporary sculpture to create a focal point in a den.

186

Take advantage of a magnificent view—here, a sleek glass-topped desk is positioned against a wall of windows overlooking the ocean.

Bedrooms

187

●

Include a writing desk and comfortable chair for letter writing in a master bedroom.

188

●

Eschew bright colors in a child's room, opting instead for a sophisticated mix of creams, tans, and taupes, spiced with accents in mustard, chili pepper, or saffron hues.

189

•

Install a fireplace in a large master bedroom and surround it with chairs or a sofa upholstered in fabrics with subtle patterns or pale solid colors.

190

•

Hang a large square mirror over a mantel to brighten and open up an already serene sitting room.

191

Include a slipcovered chaise longue near a bay window in a bedroom to create a comfortable spot for reading, napping, or just gazing out the window.

192

●

Include accents in washed-
out natural hues to promote
a peaceful atmosphere
conducive to restful sleep
in a master bedroom.

193

•

Commission the design of a
continuous headboard that
runs wall to wall and cover it
with 100-percent linen in a
flax color.

194

•

Establish a dreamy quality
in a bedroom by covering
the wall behind the bed
with smoky silvered
mirror panels.

195

Use a bamboo shade as the backdrop to a sitting area composed of two overstuffed chairs sharing a small ottoman in a master bedroom.

196

Decorate a master bedroom in soothing shades of caramel, brown, and ivory, and tuck the bed within a creamy millwork alcove.

197

Hang a mosquito net over the bed of a guest room in a tropical vacation house and cover the bed with white antique French linens.

198

Paint the walls of a bedroom a pale gray-blue and base the color palette of the accents and furnishings in the room on that hue.

199

•

Surround a poster bed with a minimalist canopy that can be pulled open and closed on both sides.

200

•

Cover doors that open onto a balcony or terrace with tall, slim shutters that can be opened to let in breezes.

Bathrooms

201

•

Combine brick-shaped tile
with Carrara marble for a
modern spa-like quality in a
bathroom featuring dark
wood and twin sinks.

202

●

Cultivate a sense of harmony and balance in a master bath by placing twin vanities— built like furniture—to face each other across the room.

203

•

Create serenity in a bathroom
by placing a sculptural tub
in front of a floor-to-ceiling
window overlooking a
water view.

Outdoor Rooms & Sunrooms

204

Construct a symmetrical pavilion for outdoor relaxing or entertaining at the far end of a pool. Install a fireplace for warmth on chilly evenings.

205

●

Add luminosity to a sunroom by painting the ceiling with silver leaf and installing shutters to control the amount of light let in.

206

●

Set a fireplace into the limestone wall of an outdoor pavilion and surround it with a mix of comfortable furniture upholstered in a creamy cotton duck.

207

Use a large coffee table as the centerpiece of a porch and as a place to display books and other collectibles.

208

Consider redoing a piece of sunroom furniture with an unexpected choice of paint or fabric—such as staining a wicker chair dark mahogany and upholstering cushions in chenille or luxurious suede—to let you see it in a whole new way.

Gardens

209

●

Enhance the splendor of a
view of wooded hills by
planting a low hedge of
Berberi's thunbergii 'Crimson
Pygmy' instead of beds of
flowers, and—if your budget
allows—incorporate a
massive abstract sculpture.

210

Line a long gravel driveway with an abundance of lavender to create a heavenly scented welcome or farewell.

211

Give a large expanse of lawn a naturally artful focal point by planting a character-filled specimen tree, such as Japanese maple.

Chapter 4 Comfortable Haven

• 222 •

• 224 •

• 230 •

• 234 •

• 237 •

• 242 •

• 245 •

• 251 •

• 253 •

• 255 •

• 256 •

• 261 •

• 265 •

• 266 •

• 269 •

THE COMFORTABLE HAVEN puts no-frills, no-fuss people at ease. Durable flooring, wash-and-wear cotton duck slipcovers, and lots of fluffy pillows and soft throws are de rigueur in its living and family rooms, and hard-to-stain countertops and easy-to-clean cabinets are standard in its kitchen. Storage spaces—from bookshelves with louvered doors to window seats with pull-out drawers—abound in every room, keeping the whole house free of clutter. Simple Roman shades add privacy and control light in bedrooms and baths. And informal pathways lead children from the house to the playhouse, while low-fuss plants keep yardwork to a minimum.

Living Spaces

212

Furnish the corner of a large living room with a sectional sofa, its thick cushions and plentiful pillows offering extra comfort.

213

●

Create a relaxed ambience
in the living room/sunporch
of a summer house with
vintage American wicker
furniture enameled
chocolate brown.

214

●

Provide low-cost comfortable seating for children in a family room by placing large, square floor cushions around a coffee table.

215

●

Give a living room a casual atmosphere with floor coverings made from a natural material, like coir or jute, in natural colors.

216

In lieu of a small, delicate
cocktail table, choose a pair
of chenille-covered square
ottomans, which can serve
as small tables, extra seating,
or a place to put up your feet.

217

•

For a clean, easy-to-maintain, and minimalist look, paint a basic brick fireplace with white high-gloss paint.

218

•

Keep a collection of books dust-free but still accessible in a tall cabinet with glass doors placed beside the fireplace.

219

Warm up the wood floors of a casual living room with a flat-weave rug in a neutral color.

220

Add variety to a symmetrically arranged living room with a mixture of round, square, and rectangular pillows, and with non-matching side tables.

221

Free up a lot of space in a small family room by hanging a flat-screen television on the wall and eliminating a bulky console.

222

Keep the family room calm—no matter how busy the activites get by using comforting and neutral tones.

Dining Rooms
& Breakfast Nooks

223

●

Create a streamlined yet
luxurious dining room by
surrounding a sculptural
monolithic dining table with
chairs upholstered in leather,
covering the ceiling with
pewter-leaf tea paper, and
installing an Art Deco
iron-and-glass chandelier.

224

•

Carve out a breakfast area
in a kitchen with four
painted-wood folding chairs
around a flea-market farm
table placed by a window.

225

●

Create an informal dining area
next to a wall of windows
with a sleek wood table and
director's chairs with
child-friendly leather seats.

226

Allow for an easy-to-host brunch for twelve by including an extendable Parsons table with a lacquered bar-top finish in a breakfast room.

227

To keep a room from getting locked into one time period, layer it with an array of styles, such as a set of 1960s pendant lighting fixtures over a French country farm table.

Kitchens & Pantries

228

Use simple, white subway tiles in a kitchen for an easy-to-clean backsplash and clean, minimalist look.

229

Paint kitchen cabinets the same pale yellow used on the walls to promote a sense of harmony in a country kitchen.

230

Warm up a big kitchen and adjoining family room with old-fashioned beadboard on the walls and ceiling.

231

Combine recessed and pendant lights on the ceiling to offer the choice of bright or atmospheric lighting.

232

Top counters with Formica edged with stainless steel and cover the high-traffic area of floor in front of the sink with a coir runner or rug.

233

Doorless shelves under the kitchen counter allow easy access to pots and pans.

234

•

Use honed semi-polished bluestone for countertops and backsplashes—it's practical and stain-resistant.

235

•

Display an eclectic and multi-hued collection of plates, teapots, and bowls on open shelves surrounding a kitchen sink.

236

Craft an eating ledge made
of Corian around a food
prep island so that the cook
can have company while
preparing meals.

237

Install open shelves over
a sink in a country kitchen for
a pretty display and to keep
kitchen items within reach.

238
●

Carve out a small work area
with a desk, a laptop, and
some drawers or shelves
and mount a mirror television
nearby to increase the function
of a kitchen.

239

Construct a plate rack over the sink for easy access. And install deep drawers on either side of the sink for storage of pots and pans and other kitchenware.

240

The top ledge of cream-colored kitchen cabinets is the perfect place to display a collection of colorful bowls.

241

Install a radiant heating system beneath a stone floor to keep feet warm in the cold winter months.

242

A two-tiered island gives the cook plenty of workspace and allows family or guests a seat near the action.

243

Add an unexpected touch of color to a professional stainless-steel range with brightly colored knobs.

244

•

Include open cabinetry with
easy-to-open deep drawers
of varying depths for pots
and pans next to the stove.

Libraries, Dens & Offices

245

Create a reading area in a cottage by placing a small table and a couple of chairs in front of a ready-made bookshelf along one wall.

246

Conceal television and stereo equipment behind the louvered doors of an entertainment center in a den.

247

Provide an expanse of extra storage in a home office by installing floor-to-ceiling bookshelves along one wall or around the whole room.

Bedrooms

248

●

Craft sweet and unique pillowcases for a guest room from vintage linen.

249

●

Cover the windows of a bedroom with woven reed shades that can be pulled up to let in the daytime sun or closed for complete privacy at night.

250

Hang a trio of decorative antique plates on either side of a guest bed to create balance and symmetry.

251

Paint the wide-planked wood floor of a bedroom white to brighten up the room, but place a rug at the foot of the bed for warmth.

252

Let a chest of drawers double as a nightstand and provide extra storage space for guests.

253

For a clean, simple look, keep bedding to a minimum and use crisp white sheets and pillowcases.

254

•

Create affordable art for a basement bedroom by framing fern fronds in a collection of flea-market frames and painting the frames in a single color.

255

●

In a guest suite, install shelving with a sliding door in front to provide a place for guests to stow away their things.

256

●

In a nursery, use an open,
cushion-topped changing table
with shelves mounted above to
provide easy access to diapers,
wipes, and other baby supplies.

257

Keep children's rooms neat by housing books, toys, and art supplies in fabric-lined baskets tucked into cubbies.

Bathrooms

258

•

Keep a powder room as
streamlined as possible
with simple hardware and
accessories, and even
exposed plumbing.

259

•

When renovating a bathroom,
place the light switch near the
door and at a level where you
would expect it to be.

260

Install a bookshelf in an over-size bath and cover the walls with a tropical leaf wallpaper.

261

Look around for keepsakes and trinkets that have a history for you to add a personal touch to a bathroom.

262

Porcelain floor tiles are durable and inexpensive.

Outdoor Rooms
& Sunrooms

263

Place a pair of colorful
Thai silk or cotton pillows
on a porch swing to promote
a lazy afternoon of relaxation
and appreciation of the view.

264

•

Keep children's sports gear out
of sight and in order by hanging
vintage lockers—found at a flea
market or antique store—on a
wall in the garage.

265

Toss a throw over a table on a sunporch to give a casual country air to an al fresco table setting.

266

Let teak patio furniture weather naturally to an appealing silvery hue that blends into the outdoor environment.

267

Place two or three Adirondack chairs at the end of a dock as a place to sit back and enjoy a summer sunrise or sunset, depending on which direction it's facing.

Gardens

268

To preserve the lawn, install a series of stepping stones along a high-traffic path through a garden.

269

Set up pairs of lounge chairs—topped with thick cushions for extra comfort— along the sides of a pool in a lushly tropical setting.

270

•

Plant angelica and wild
buttercups in an herb garden
near a picket gate.

271

●

Create a path through a
side yard with different-sized
pieces of weathered flagstone
in a non-linear arrangement.

272

Place a collection of bistro
chairs around a table beneath
an impossibly romantic canopy of
fragrant wisteria.

273

A whimsical candle-lantern over
an outdoor dining table can be
magical for evening meals.

Chapter 5 Natural Abode

THE NATURAL ABODE is best suited for nature enthusiasts, environmentalists, and lovers of the great outdoors. This home's living, working, and eating spaces are likely to be rooms with large windows and sensational views. They're also inclined to be filled with recycled or eco-conscious materials—reclaimed wood floors, river-rock walls, organic cotton sheets. These houses invariably harmonize with their settings, fitting in with the landscape like trees in a park. And their surroundings are often naturalistic, yet laced with stone benches, fire pits, or wraparound terraces, enabling their inhabitants to commune with their surroundings and nature's splendors.

Living Spaces

274

●

Install a stone, marble, or tile floor, and use nontoxic grout as a first step toward creating an environmentally friendly living room.

275

Bring the outdoors indoors by scattering a variety of plants and flowers in an open living/dining space.

276

Surround a modern fireplace in a renovated rustic structure with bamboo and cover the floor with slate.

277

Take advantage of a striking view by installing a floor-to-ceiling window wall along one side of a living room.

278

Decorate a living room in a house in a California desert setting with furnishings and accents made of natural organic materials and a palette that complements the landscape.

279

Display a pottery collection on a hand-carved pine mantel.

280

Hang a chandelier made of naturally shed elk horns in front of a stone fireplace in the great room of a getaway house.

281

Create a mantel shelf with solid untreated walnut or other hardwood.

282

Make the most of a tropical setting by surrounding a living room with doors that open on all sides.

283

Top an expansive brick fireplace with an old wood beam for a rustic look.

284

Place a vase of tall, cheerful sunflowers in front of a fireplace in the warmer months.

285

Construct a glass enclosure to form a protected living room within the shell of an old barn that's been converted into a house.

Dining Rooms & Breakfast Nooks

286

Have a custom-designed table built from solid mahogany and protect it with a water-based sealant.

287

Choose upholstered dining room chairs filled with natural cotton or wool rather than synthetic polyurethane foam.

288

●

Top an outdoor dining table with natural elements, here tall wooden candle holders carved in the shape of tree branches.

289

Top dining room chairs with linen slipcovers for easy cleaning and so that you can change the look of the room with new slipcovers.

290

Place a flowering plant potted in an urn in front of a mirror for double the greenery.

291

Surround a dining room with floor-to-ceiling glass walls so that it appears to float in a forested setting.

Kitchens & Pantries

292

•

Construct open shelves on open supports to permit views into an adjoining room and an ocean or river view beyond.

293

Use reclaimed wood to cover the floor of a charming country kitchen for a rustic look and feel.

294

Divide a large kitchen into distinct rooms with area rugs that both contrast with and complement each other.

295

Top an island with a trio of small potted citrus trees to add a tropical, cheery touch to a kitchen.

296

Lend warmth with a mix of natural materials, including both dark and light wood.

297

Create an eye-catching backsplash using brightly colored tiles in a small kitchen with little natural light.

298

●

Give a modern kitchen rich, earthy appeal with stark mahogany cabinetry, narrow open shelves, and limestone floors.

299

●

Install a pivoting window over the kitchen sink to add a bounce of light from an adjoining room.

Libraries, Dens & Offices

300

Call attention to a magnificent view from a den by framing glass doors with vibrant red floor-length draperies made of a natural material like wool gabardine.

301

Add a unique touch to a den by placing a dramatic lamp on a side table between a sofa and small chair.

302

Fill a cabinet with an artfully
arranged collection of shells
and coral, and other keepsakes.

303

A wall that bows a bit or a floor
that has settled will make an
old room feel graceful rather
than brand new.

304

•

Enjoy natural beauty while you work by placing a console and X-based ottoman in front of a window overlooking an amazing view.

305

•

Exchange a bulky computer for a sleek laptop in a home office to avoid clutter.

Bedrooms

306

Top a bed with sheets made
from 100-percent organic
cotton or silk and blankets of
natural undyed wool.

307

Indulge guests by framing a
spectacular landscape with
a large window in a guest room.

308

Add warmth to a bedroom by topping an ornately designed wicker bed with plaid wool linens.

309

Use traditional milk paint to avoid the effects of harmful volatile organic compounds in a guest bedroom.

310

•

Create a tree-house atmosphere in a contemporary bedroom by covering walls with grass cloth and installing ebony-stained beadboard on a vaulted ceiling.

311

•

Avoid down pillows or comforters because they offer a haven for dust mites.

312

Bring the outdoors in by covering the floor of a bedroom with slate that matches an exterior patio beyond a glass window wall.

313

Hide steel support beams behind weathered wood for a more natural look in an open bedroom with sparse, modern furniture.

Bathrooms

314

Use natural materials—such as limestone walls, 100-percent cotton towels, and linen shades—in a bathroom.

315

Add a view of the outdoors with a window over a bathtub, but mount a roman shade for privacy.

316

Put a charming antique farm table into service as a counter for a basin in a country-style bathroom.

317

Use a handwoven basket to stash fresh towels. Store it on the bathroom counter or on the floor next to the bathtub.

Outdoor Rooms & Sunrooms

318

•

Build an upstairs outdoor deck
near—and partially under—
the roof of a house.

319

Accent the rustic charm of a renovated barn with a totally modern staircase leading from a stone patio.

320

Make the most of a creekside view by orienting an enclosed sunroom with generous expanses of picture windows toward the water.

321

Commune with nature on a chilly day and stay warm at the same time by installing a kiva fireplace within a covered open-air portal.

322

Provide a comfortable place from which to enjoy a view by building a deep, covered loggia and placing an array of thickly cushioned chairs on it.

323

Plant wisteria to shade a dining area loggia from the setting sun and fill the air with magical scent.

324

If you serve ribs or lobster at a summer picnic or barbeque, float some violets or wildflowers in the finger bowls that will be needed.

325

•

Define the entrance to a
pueblo-style house with antique
Mexican pine doors and Spanish
Colonial–style lanterns.

326

•

Design an entrance courtyard
to ease the transition between
indoors and outdoors, and to
provide a private outdoor haven.

327

•

Craft a deck from ipe, an
exceptionally durable Brazilian
hardwood that ages gracefully
and that goes perfectly with a
gorgeous ocean view.

Gardens

328

Construct an open
Anglo-Japanese–inspired
gazebo to provide a quiet
spot for contemplation in a
naturalistic garden.

329

If you have a stream that is prone to flooding on your property, line its banks with stones found nearby or purchased at a local nursery.

330

Design a house that blends in with the landscape and reflects the region where it is constructed.

331

Conserve natural resources and minimize impact on the landscape by converting an old barn into a modern weekend house.

332

Treat yourself to a visual feast by planting a border of flowers and grasses, such as purple *Aster novae-angliae* 'Violetta' and silvery pink *Miscanthus* 'Flamingo,' that change colors with the arrival of a new season.

333

Plant impatiens along a winding path of closely spaced stones leading to a formal main garden.

334

•

Create meandering paths
through a wooded property
to encourage long walks and
appreciation of nature.

335

•

Add character to a garden wall
in the Southwest with a pair of
antique hand-wrought wooden
doors at the entrance.

336

Place a rough-hewn birdbath in a shady corner of a garden as both a work of art and a place for birds to drink and play.

337

Encourage blue aquilegias and *Euphorbia amygdaloides* 'Rubra' to seed themselves in a garden pergola for a wild, overgrown look.

338

•

Landscape the grounds of
an old stone house with
indigenous stone, plants,
and trees.

339

•

When renovating an old
house, reuse as many of the
original roof tiles, bricks,
and beams as possible.

340

●

Introduce a sculptural touch to a desert landscape with aged terra-cotta olive jars that echo the palette of the natural surroundings.

341

Keep the colors of flowering plants on a terrace subtle so as not to compete with a stunning view of a valley.

342

Construct a fire pit on the upper level of a tiered garden and install a long, concrete bench, topping it with plenty of cushions to provide comfort during late-night gatherings.

Chapter 6   Bold Domain

• 338 •

• 339 •

• 342 •

• 348 •

• 351 •

• 359 •

• 360 •

• 363 •

• 371 •

• 377 •

• 381 •

• 384 •

• 386 •

• 393 •

• 395 •

FOR CONTEMPORARY CULTURE MAVENS, technophiles, and those who love everything cutting-edge, there's no place like the Bold Domain. Its living spaces flow into its dining spaces, and both are probably filled with gutsy modern art, vibrant color, and conversation-piece furniture. A large, flat-screen television is probably the centerpiece of the family room, where a Tommi Parzinger lamp might stand next to a Jean-Michel Frank sofa and an animal-print rug covers the floor. Private spaces have attitude too, including children's rooms, where framed vintage French posters might add color to the walls or a hot-pink canopy might cover the bed of a budding princess. Outdoor rooms and gardens are sleek and languid with chaise longues and ultramodern party lights.

Living Spaces

343

•

Make a bold statement in an entrance hall by painting walls purple and enlivening them with a quartet of colorful abstract paintings.

344

Let unusual artwork or collectibles, such as a pair of 19th-century Chinese cranes, inspire a visual narrative.

345

Create a dramatic staircase with Honduran mahogany paneling and Chippendale-inspired fretwork rails.

346

Bring an exotic touch to an otherwise understated living room with zebra-patterned cowhide rugs.

347

Flank a glamorous bar table in a family room with a pair of flare-arm chairs upholstered in pale pink linen.

348

Cover the floor of a family room with a white shag rug to add texture and comfort.

349

•

Give a vaulted family room an air of stylish glamour by suspending a pendant fixture with an oversize modern Italian lampshade from the ceiling.

350

Bring a playful touch to a sitting room by displaying a collection of contemporary art. Here, bird paintings by the artist Robert Flynn hang over a white sofa.

351

Let a red-cushioned coffee table inspire an array of bold accents in a comfortable and inviting family room.

352

Consolidate your electronic devices on a universal remote control, which can coordinate the television and stereo and even draw the curtains and dim the lighting.

353

•

Cover the walls of a living
room with a zebra-stripe
wallpaper but tone down the
look by hanging traditional
floral paintings and a pretty
oval mirror.

354

Carve out an alluring seating niche in a living room with a corner banquette covered in chartreuse moleskin and pillows made from brightly colored Indian silks.

355

Clad a slanted ceiling in mahogany and accentuate it with a monolithic limestone fireplace that rises to the full height of a living room.

356

Install rain-sensor windows or skylights that can detect moisture and automatically close before the carpet and furniture become soaked.

357

Set off clean, geometric furniture in a neutral room with a gutsy work of art, here an abstract painting by Ed Moses.

358

•

Cover a bergère chair in a
vibrant multicolored stripe
to add color and personality
to a formal living room.

Dining Rooms & Breakfast Nooks

359

●

Mount an abstract work of art
from the 1930s or '40s on one
wall of a dining room over a
sideboard, here a mid-century
Tommi Parzinger.

360

Surround a wood-grained Formica table with chairs upholstered in dazzling white patent leather and hang a funky chandelier over the table to complete the look.

361

Set off white wainscoting in a dining room by painting the walls and ceiling a glossy coral and adding a band of framed sepia photographs.

362

A blue-tiled fireplace matches the seat coverings and table linens in this bright and cheerful dining area. Bold, mismatching fabrics are pulled together by their blue color palette.

363

Set a lighthearted tone in a dining room by displaying items with visual panache. Shown here is a polka-dot Hermès vase.

364

Add energy to a dining room by mixing pieces from different eras, such as the modernist Eero Saarinen table and an 18th-century chest shown here.

365

•

Install an upholstered
banquette in a dining room
and top with lots of fluffy
pillows to create a comfortable
spot for predinner cocktails.

366

•

Install a scene-control lighting
system that can provide varying
levels of light in different
rooms—or on specific objects,
such as artwork—with the flip
of a switch.

367

Enrich an austere dining room with a graphic piece of modern art and a striking lighting fixture such as this 1940s Italian mercury glass chandelier.

368

•

Light fixtures can provide just the color accent necessary to add excitement and warmth to a room.

Kitchens & Pantries

369

Add charm to a French-inspired kitchen by having a whimsical trompe l'oeil painted above your modern-retro, professional stove.

370

•

Install a custom-designed island with an ultrathick slab of marble that projects out to form an enormous tabletop with room for five.

371

•

For a dramatic and somewhat formal effect, put a black-and-white diamond backsplash behind a stainless-steel stove.

372

Give a kitchen a modern look that's not sterile with a mix of Douglas fir cabinetry, oak floors, and stainless-steel countertops.

373

Install a sound system with a central control and speakers in different rooms so that you can hear classical music in the kitchen and R&B in the family room.

374

Surround a kitchen island
with white faux-bamboo bar
stools and top it with a
playful ceramic planter.

375

Strike a bold note over a long kitchen island with Artemide's Omega pendant lamps—reissued from the 1960s—and surround it with ultramodern stainless-steel bar stools.

376

Make the most of the space in a narrow, urban kitchen by building cabinets all the way up to the ceiling.

377

Hang a large collection of copper pots near a gas cooktop for convenience and to enhance the decor.

378

Spice up a modern kitchen with a tall mosaic backsplash of tiles in zesty hues.

Libraries, Dens & Offices

379

Paint the interior of a
tall bookshelf in a color
that contrasts with the
walls of an office while
complementing other
pieces in the room.

380

•

Flank a plasma television mounted above a fireplace in a den with a pair of primitive masks and cover the fireplace with a bold one-of-a-kind screen.

381

•

Connect all your household computers on a single, preferably wireless, home network to streamline record keeping and file sharing. This way you can create a budget spreadsheet on your computer in the den and later access it from your laptop on the terrace or in bed.

382

Go bold in an office with dark wood-paneled walls by combining richly patterned fabrics that both complement and contrast with one another.

383

In a small home office, pair a round, overscale contemporary pedestal table with an Eames Management chair in a bold color and paint the ceiling with tan and white stripes.

Bedrooms

384

Upholster a striking headboard
that extends beyond the width
of the bed and around both
side tables in trapunto with
nailhead detailing.

385

●

Bring a touch of glamour to a guest room with gilt-trimmed furnishings and accessories.

386

●

Open up a bedroom painted a rich color by leaning an oversized mirror that nearly reaches the ceiling against a bare wall.

387

Add zest to a guest room with bright yellow linens and some modern art and furniture.

388

Break from tradition and place the head of a bed against the middle of a bay window.

389

Upholster a headboard in bold horizontal stripes and use framed vintage movie posters as art in a teen's room.

390

Pair hot pink and neon green—or other favorite colors of a particular child—in various shades to make a girl's room bright and cheerful.

391

Give punch to a teen's room with bright color, a checkerboard floor, a cozy tucked-away window seat, and a lamp made from an antique mannequin's head.

392

Create a canopy that suggests
a safari tent over the bed in
a boy's bedroom. Add to the
theme with an animal-print
rug on the floor at the end
of the bed.

393

Drape fabric with a strong graphic pattern behind a colorful headboard and have custom bed linens made to complement both.

394

Top a chest of drawers in a master bedroom with a colorful pair of 1960s porcelain foo dogs.

395

Upholster a headboard in the same floral-print fabric as the bedskirt and tone down the look with simple linens in solid colors.

Bathrooms

396

Install an undulating two-sink vanity and a supersize steel tub in a bathroom for a modern, sleek look.

397

•

Install a concrete shower tub—with a built-in bench—alongside a wall of swimming pool tiles for a bold, clean look.

398

Add Hollywood glamour to a master bathroom with iridescent glass mosaic tiles in an oversize shower with multiple shower heads.

399

Add a vanity to a bathroom so that makeup doesn't have to be applied while leaning over a sink.

Outdoor Rooms & Sunrooms

400

Build a pool house inspired
by the style of a Japanese
teahouse and decorated with
plenty of outdoor furniture.

401
●

Craft a contemporary pool
pavilion on a deck overlooking
the ocean by stretching sailcloth
over a steel-framed cube.

402
●

Surround two sides of a master
bedroom suite with a covered
terrace that overlooks an
expansive view on one side
and a pool on the other.

403

•

Contain an open-air porch with grommetted curtain panels that can be opened and closed with ease.

404

•

Position four custom chairs with thick cushions covered in brightly colored fabric around a narrow coffee table on a sun porch.

405

Set some brightly painted French iron spoon chairs at either end of a sturdy teak farm table on a covered terrace.

406

Construct a dramatic fireplace at one end of a patio, place a coffee table in front of it, and surround it with stylish teak sofas and chairs.

Gardens

407

●

Create a splendid vista with arched hedges that lead the eye from one part of a garden to another.

408

Recreate the south of France on a rooftop terrace with a painted latticework and foamy herbs.

409

Plant highly scented plants like lavender, rosemary, and wisteria for a garden that will smell like heaven.

410

Construct a blue-bottomed infinity pool on an elevated terrace overlooking the desert hills.

411

Frame a sunken pool in an organic shape with massive, rough limestone rocks and palm trees to give the feeling of swimming on a tropical island.

Chapter 7 The Welcoming Home

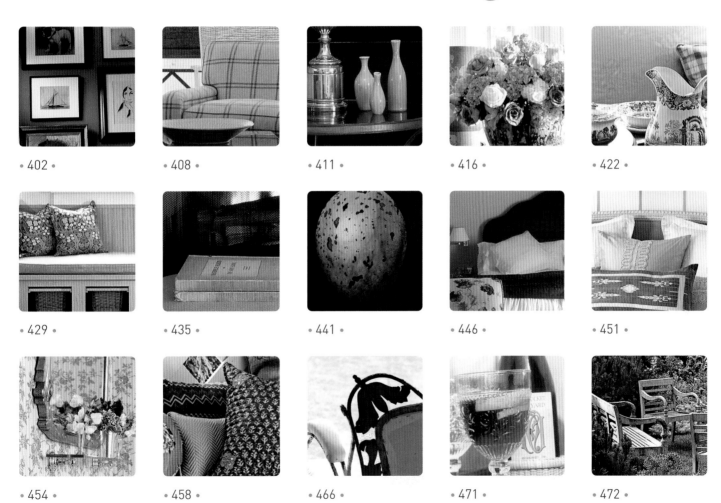

THE WELCOMING HOME is all about comfort. Although the furniture and accessories in its living and eating areas may be new, their shapes and colors are familiar. Overstuffed sofas and chairs encourage family and friends to sit back and stay awhile. An antique or two in the living room brings out memories of an earlier generation, while a zesty paint color in a family room indulges the sensibilities of an emerging one. Guest rooms are equipped with all the comforts of home, while the master suite is the ultimate haven, with floor-length draperies, plush carpet, and upholstered reading chairs. A swing on a covered porch, picnic tables and cushioned chairs on an expansive patio, or lounge chairs in a cozy cabana offer multiple outdoor rest spots.

Living Spaces

412

Enhance the relaxed air in a beach cottage hallway by hanging framed vintage posters with seaside themes on the wall.

413

Create an inviting window seat by topping a hidden radiator with an upholstered cushion and fluffy pillows.

414

Instead of placing a coffee table in front of a sofa in a living room, use a large upholstered ottoman.

415

Toss down-filled pillows onto a pair of wing chairs in a living room for added comfort.

416

Add character and warmth to a stairwell by painting walls in earthy tones and installing cream-painted wainscoting.

417

Make a large, sunny room even more inviting by upholstering a sofa and chairs in plush textured fabrics and buttery leather, adding plenty of pillows.

418

Create coziness in a large living room by setting up two distinct seating areas.

419

Pile plenty of soft blankets in drawers beneath a window seat in a family room for easy access.

420

Carve out a cozy spot for kids in a cottage by creating a napping nook atop a platform of pull-out drawers for storing blankets.

421

•

Create a comfy spot to read near a window with an upholstered cushion, a bolster, a soft throw, and a side table for books and a glass of wine.

422

•

Establish a sense of openness by dividing rooms with partial-height walls or glass-paned doors to allow a visual connection from one room to another.

423

Brighten a living room by upholstering overstuffed chairs in a windowpane check and pairing them with a custom rug inspired by a Josef Albers painting.

424

Place a few pieces of folk art or craft work from a flea market or fair on a fireplace mantel in an otherwise sparsely accented room.

425

•

Add color to an open, three-level foyer with an abstract wall hanging along one staircase.

426

•

Give energy to a traditional living room by using a fresh, youthful palette that is reflected in the walls, fabrics, and accents.

427

●

Bring a fresh twist to an
all-American palette of red,
white, and blue with Asian
furnishings, prints, and
accents in a bright sunroom.

428

●

Cover the walls of a children's sitting room with large-scale hemp gingham and upholster a commodious chaise longue with a child-friendly acrylic fabric.

429

●

Paint the wood floor of a small living room white to make the space seem larger.

Dining Rooms & Breakfast Nooks

430

•

Create a casual dining space in a great room with a long picnic bench pulled up next to a simple French farm table.

431

Give a youthful air to a traditional dining room by covering chair seats with parrot-green-and-white—checkered skirts.

432

Surround a dining table with high-backed upholstered chairs for comfort and to add a decadent touch of formality to the room.

433

●

Enrich a country table setting with a centerpiece of hydrangea, roses, and poppies in a wooden box and candle tapers placed in clear vases.

434

•

Mount a pair of mismatched tole trays above a fireplace for a decorative touch in a breakfast room adjoining a sunny kitchen.

435

•

Create a casual eating area off a kitchen by pushing an Arts and Crafts table next to a banquette and adding a couple of chairs for plenty of seating.

436

Create an inviting breakfast nook near a bay window with a lazy Susan tray, benches, and plenty of cushions covered in yellow, blue, and white fabrics.

437

Include a couple of upholstered stools, or taborets, along with a set of chairs around a dining room table to add a dash of personality.

438

•

Use a mix of seating—
a cushion-topped bench,
high-backed armchairs,
and side chairs—around
a dining table for an
inviting ambience.

439

Add zing to a breakfast nook by applying black toile wallpaper above tall white paneling and painting the back of inset shelves lime green.

Kitchens & Pantries

440

•

Keep a small kitchen bright
and airy by positioning
wall-mounted cabinets out of
the way below ceiling level.

441

•

Create a country feeling in
a kitchen with hardwood
floors, painted cabinetry, and
butter-yellow walls.

442

To vary the effects of lighting, incorporate a variety of fixture types—including pendants and under-the-cabinet lighting—and include dimmers.

443

Bring sophistication to a country-style kitchen with marble countertops, also used on a long kitchen island.

444

•

Paint the walls of a kitchen
a bright yellow to create a
cheery, welcoming atmosphere.

445

•

If your kitchen is short on counter
space, add an oversized island in
the center of the room to give you
more prep room.

446

Install a comfortable window seat in a kitchen for guests and place storage baskets below.

447

If you are concerned about stains, choose easy-to-clean quartz or granite instead of marble to top an island.

448

Add a long runner in the high-traffic area of a narrow kitchen to create a soft, cozy feel.

449

●

Create an open kitchen that has it all—extensive food prep space, an eating area, and a place nearby for family to sit and watch television.

450

●

Personalize your kitchen with displays of majolica pitchers, ironstone bowls, or ceramic teapots.

Libraries, Dens & Offices

451

•

Instead of track lighting, which draws the eye up, use an interesting table lamp with a curvy base on a desk in a home office with a low ceiling.

452

•

A lot of clutter can be contained behind the glass doors of a cabinet while also providing a delightful visual display.

453

•

Transform a cluttered library into an inviting haven by painting shelves and cabinets a pale sage-green, covering windows with soft shades, and adding comfortable wing chairs.

454

•

Install wall-to-wall carpet in a library for soft comfort underfoot and to cultivate a quiet environment perfect for reading.

455

Whip up some cushions made from vintage silk scarves to toss on a sofa for extra comfort.

456

Position a wing chair, ottoman, and chaise longue near a fireplace in a den for plenty of fireside seating during the chilly months.

457

Turn the top floor of a three-story house into an inviting homework/media room for teenage children.

458

Put down an equestrian-themed rug and add matching pillows on the sofa and chairs to keep a library feeling fun and family-friendly.

459

●

Upholster a pair of chairs in front of an enormous brick fireplace in a cozy study with a cheery striped fabric and make floor-length draperies from a sunny toile.

Bedrooms

460

Paint the walls of a country
bedroom with twin beds a
pale violet-blue for a fresh
and serene feeling.

461

If you like to read in bed, be
sure to have an extra-big
pillow to prop up and avoid a
wrought-iron headboard.

462

•

Gown a pair of beds in a guest room with canopies made with gathered fabric suspended from a corbel mounted on the wall.

463

Add comfort to a bedroom
by covering the floor with
a colorful and sumptuous rug.

464

Create a cozy spot for reading
in a bedroom by placing an
upholstered chair, a side table,
and a reading lamp in one corner.

465

•

Bring charm to a guest room with sheer curtain panels, an upholstered headboard, and a ruffled bed skirt.

466

Place two beds right together—
instead of separating with a
table—to create a cozy
guest bedroom.

467

Very pale blue walls in a
guest bedroom creates a
peaceful atmosphere that
promotes relaxation.

468

•

Inject color and comfort in a
guest room by painting the
walls and headboard in vibrant
hues. Include a matching pair
of cozy upholstered chairs and
a tea table to create an area
where family and friends can sit
and take in a garden view.

469

●

Fill a guest room with
old-fashioned warmth by
covering the walls with a
sunny patterned fabric that
matches the upholstery on
a daybed.

470

Keep a large antique armoire
made of dark wood from
overpowering a bedroom by
choosing one that has mirror
on its doors.

471

•

Cover the walls and ceiling of a cozy attic bedroom in red-and-white toile and cover the bed with white linens.

472

•

Place a small writing desk in a window nook with a view.

473

Cover a padded headboard with striped taffeta and use neutral fabrics to fashion a luxurious canopy over the head of the bed.

474

Place a velvet-upholstered sofa at the foot of a bed and top it with opulent pillows and a boldly patterned throw.

475

Fill an antique glass bottle with branches of quince to create a stunning focal point in a guest bedroom.

476

Cover the walls and vaulted ceiling of a guest bedroom with a cheerful floral wallpaper to create a cozy welcome.

Bathrooms

477

For soft lighting in a
bathroom, flank a mirror
over the sink with sconces
sporting fabric shades.

478

Add charm to a high-ceilinged guest bath with a floral custom-designed wallpaper.

479

Add a touch of spring to a powder room with potted flowering plants and miniature bouquets of fresh flowers.

480

•

A pulled work tablecloth is graphic and yet old-fashioned as a shower curtain lined with lime-colored fabric in a cozy bathroom.

Outdoor Rooms
& Sunrooms

481

●

Set up a cozy spot in a sunroom
by placing a lacquered cocktail
table in front of a vintage daybed
in a window corner.

482

●

Cover the floor of a sunroom
with a boldly patterned rug
that is echoed in the geometric
art painted on the doors of
an armoire.

483

•

Toss a bevy of colorful silk
and cotton pillows of all
shapes and sizes on a deep-
cushioned iron daybed on a
covered porch.

484

•

Install a fanciful candle
chandelier on the ceiling of a
covered terrace for evening
enjoyment or a bit of
romance.

485

●

Set up multiple seating areas on an expansive pea gravel patio—perfect for gatherings on warm summer nights.

486

●

Install a fireplace on an expansive porch to provide warmth on chilly evenings.

487

●

Hang a cedar swing from the ceiling of a screened-in porch for relaxing with a glass of tea or wine.

488

●

Add personality to a porch
with a row of rocking
chairs and a band of modern
pendant lamps covered in
striped-fabric shades.

489

•

Drill a hole in the bottom of an old ceramic hog trough and convert it into a sink in a garden potting shed.

490

●

Create a multipurpose relaxation zone in a sunroom by including Anglo-Indian cane chairs, surrounding two or three sides of the room with a cushion-topped banquette, and pulling up a table and dining chairs along one portion of the banquette.

491

●

Install a wood stove to warm up a large sunroom even in the coldest winter months.

492

●

Position a pair of cushioned
1930s French iron chairs
and side table on a terrace
overlooking a formal garden
and swimming pool.

Gardens

493

●

Flank the front door of an
ivy-covered stone house with
agapanthus planted in pots
that can be brought indoors
when the weather turns cold.

494

Construct a wooden swing set and fort for children of all ages in the backyard.

495

In springtime, the fallen petals from blossoming trees will create a beautiful carpet of color on an outstretched lawn.

496

Use fine linens for a rustic picnic—the napkins won't blow away in the wind, and the juxtaposition is charming.

497

Toss a queen-size blanket or sheet on the sand to define an area for a picnic along the shore facing a summer house.

498

Press matching dish towels into service as napkins for an informal beachside brunch.

499

Cultivate a garden in keeping with the character of your house and any other structures on your property.

500

Line a garden path made from different-sized stepping stones with lamb's ears and arabis.

Photo Credits

Page 5: *Frances Janisch*

Page 6: *Eric Piasecki*

Page 8: *Karyn R. Millet*

Page 9: *Tria Giovan*

Page 10: *Gordon Beall*

Page 11: *Carlos Domenech*

Page 12: *Dominique Vorillon*

Page 14: *Eric Piasecki*

Page 16: *Eric Piasecki*

Page 19: *Gordon Beall*

Page 20: *Eric Piasecki*

Page 21: *Gordon Beall*

Page 22: *Gordon Beall*

Page 23: *Don Freeman*

Page 24: *Gordon Beall*

Page 25: *Gordon Beall*

Page 26: *Antoine Bootz*

Page 27: *Antoine Bootz*

Page 28: *Tria Giovan*

Page 29: *Thibault Jeanson*

Page 30: *Eric Piasecki*

Page 31: *John Gould Bessler*

Page 32: *Antoine Bootz*

Page 33: *Don Freeman*

Page 34: *Oberto Gili*

Page 35: *Roger Davies*

Page 36: *Thibault Jeanson*

Page 37: *Don Freeman*

Page 38: *Eric Piasecki*

Page 39: *Tim Clinch*

Page 40: *Hugh Stewart*

Page 41: *Tria Giovan*

Page 42: *Tim Street-Porter*

Page 43: *Ann Stratton*

Page 44: *Don Freeman*

Page 45: *Hugh Stewart*

Page 46: *Jeremy Samuelson*

Page 47: *John Ellis*

Page 48: *Don Freeman*

Page 49: *Roger Davies*

Page 50: *Thibault Jeanson*

Page 51: *Jeremy Samuelson*

Page 52: *Brendan Paul and Darrin Haddad*

Page 53: *Roger Davies*

Page 54: *Don Freeman*

Page 55: *Gordon Beall*

Page 56: *Jacques Dirand*

Page 57: *John M. Hall*

Page 58: *Eric Piasecki*

Page 59: *Tim Clinch*

Page 60: *Tim Clinch*

Page 61: *Don Freeman*

Page 62: *Tim Street-Porter*

Page 63: *Don Freeman*

Page 64: *Thibault Jeanson*

Page 65: *Eric Piasecki*

Page 66: *Tim Clinch*

Page 67: *Eric Piasecki*

Page 68: *Thibault Jeanson*

Page 69: *Thibault Jeanson*

Page 70: *Simon Upton*

Page 71: *Don Freeman*

Page 73: *Fernando Bengoechea*

Page 74: *Don Freeman*

Page 75: *John Ellis*

Page 76: *Tim Street-Porter*

Page 77: *Don Freeman*

Page 78: *Jeremy Samuelson*

Page 79: *Frances Janisch*

Page 80: *Thibault Jeanson*

Page 81: *Tim Street-Porter*

Page 82: *Leah Fasten*

Page 83: *Don Freeman*

Page 84: *Oberto Gili*

Page 85: *Tim Clinch*

Page 86: *Ann Stratton*

Page 87: *Tria Giovan*

Page 88: *John M. Hall*

Page 89: *Mick Hales*

Page 90: *John M. Hall*

Page 91: *Nina Bramhall*

Page 92: *Gordon Beall*

Page 93: *John M. Hall*

Page 94: *Tim Street-Porter*

Page 95: *Vivian Russell*

Page 96: *John M. Hall*

Page 98: *Vicente Wolf*

Page 101: *Eric Piasecki*

Page 102: *Gordon Beall*

Page 103: *Tim Beddow*

Page 104: *Eric Piasecki*

Page 105: *Eric Piasecki*

Page 106: *Simon Upton*

Page 107: *Tim Street-Porter*

Page 108: *Grey Crawford*

Page 109: *Roger Davies*

Page 110: *Eric Piasecki*

Page 111: *Oberto Gili*

Page 112: *Eric Piasecki*

Page 113: *Ray Kachatorian*

Page 114: *Roger Davies*

Page 115: *Roger Davies*

Page 116: *Simon Upton*

Page 117: *Ray Kachatorian*

Page 118: *Tim Beddow*

Page 119: *J. Savage Gibson*

Page 120: *Oberto Gili*

Page 121: *Eric Piasecki*

Page 122: *Eric Piasecki*

Page 123: *Jonn Coolidge*

Page 124: *Tim Beddow*

Page 125: *Tria Giovan*

Page 126: *Lizzie Himmel*

Page 127: *John Gould Bessler*

Page 128: *Eric Piasecki*

Page 129: *Gordon Beall*

Page 130: *Gordon Beall*

Page 131: *Eric Roth*

Page 132: *Oberto Gili*

Page 133: *Kerri McCaffety*

Page 135: *Simon Upton*

Page 136: *Tim Beddow*

Page 137: *Eric Piasecki*

Page 138: *Gordon Beall*

Page 140: *Tria Giovan*

Page 141: *Oberto Gili*

Page 142: *Ray Kachatorian*

Page 143: *Vicente Wolf*

Page 144: *Simon Upton*

Page 146: *Tim Beddow*

Page 147: *John Gould Bessler*

Page 148: *Laura Resen*

Page 149: *Thibault Jeanson*

Page 150: *Melanie Acevedo*

Page 151: *Tim Beddow*

Page 152: *Grey Crawford*

Page 153: *Gordon Beall*

Page 154: *Eric Piasecki*

Page 155: *Kerri McCaffety*

Page 156: *Mick Hales*

Page 157: *Eric Crichton/Corbis*

Page 158: *Gordon Beall*

Page 161: *Timothy Bell*

Page 162: *Grey Crawford*

Page 164: *Jonn Coolidge*

Page 165: *Vicente Wolf*

Page 166: *Jack Thompson*

Page 167: *Eric Boman*

Page 168: *Roger Davies*

Page 169: *Carlos Domenech*

Page 170: *Jack Thompson*

Page 171: *Gordon Beall*

Page 172: *Steve Freihon*

Page 173: *Tria Giovan*

Page 174: *Jack Thompson*

Page 175: *Tria Giovan*

Page 176: *Roger Davies*

Page 177: *Christopher Baker*

Page 178: *Jonn Coolidge*

Page 179: *Vicente Wolf*

Page 180: *Christopher Baker*

Page 181: *Carlos Domenech*

Page 182: *Tria Giovan*

Page 183: *Jack Thompson*

Page 184: *John Gould Bessler*

Page 185: *Peter Murdock*

Page 186: *John Gould Bessler*

Page 187: *Roger Davies*

Page 188: *John M. Hall*

Page 189: *Eric Piasecki*

Page 190: *Jack Thompson*

Page 191: *Gordon Beall*

Page 192: *Grey Crawford*

Page 193: *Jonn Coolidge*

Page 194: *Gordon Beall*

Page 195: *Jack Thompson*

Page 196: *Gordon Beall*

Page 197: *Tria Giovan*

Page 198: *Karyn R. Millet*

Page 200: *Vicente Wolf*

Page 201: *Jack Thompson*

Page 202: *Karyn R. Millet*

Page 203: *Roger Davies*

Page 204: *Eric Piasecki*

Page 205: *Gordon Beall*

Page 206: *Oberto Gili*

Page 207: *Grey Crawford*

Page 208: *John Gould Bessler*

Page 210: *Oberto Gili*

Page 211: *Jack Thompson*

Page 212: *Roger Davies*

Page 213: *Jack Thompson*

Page 214: *Jack Thompson*

Page 215: *Mick Hales*

Page 216: *Tim Beddow*

Page 217: *Mick Hales*

Page 218: *Gordon Beall*

Page 221: *William Waldron*

Page 222: *Christopher Baker*

Page 223: *Brendan Paul*

Page 225: *Hugh Stewart*

Page 226: *Timothy Bell*

Page 227: *Steve Freihon*

Page 228: *Erik Kvalsvik*

Page 230: *Paul Whicheloe*

Page 231: *Paul Whicheloe*

Page 232: *Grey Crawford*

Page 233: *Don Freeman*

Page 234: *Antoine Bootz*

Page 236: *Grey Crawford*

Page 237: *Laura Moss*

Page 238: *Karyn R. Millet*

Page 240: *Christopher Baker*

Page 241: *Erik Kvalsvik*

Page 242: *Lambros
    Photography Inc.*

Page 243: *Kerri McCaffety*

Page 244: *Ellen McDermott*

Page 245: *J. Savage Gibson*

Page 246: *Peter Murdock*

Page 248: *Peter Murdock*

Page 249: *Joshua McHugh*

Page 250: *J. Savage Gibson*

Page 251: *Ben Duggan*

Page 252: *Brendan Paul*

Page 253: *J. Savage Gibson*

Page 254: *Don Freeman*

Page 255: *Steve Freihon*

Page 256: *Brendan Paul*

Page 257: *Gordon Beall*

Page 258: *Fred Lyon*

Page 259: *Fred Lyon*

Page 260: *Gordon Beall*

Page 261: *Jeff McNamara*

Page 262: *Ray Kachatorian*

Page 263: *Gordon Beall*

Page 264: *Hugh Stewart*

Page 265: *Christopher Baker*

Page 266: *Christopher Baker*

Page 268: *Roger Davies*

Page 269: *Grey Crawford*

Page 270: *Vivian Russell*

Page 272: *Gordon Beall*

Page 273: *Ray Kachatorian*

Page 274: *Erik Kvalsvik*

Page 277: *Edmund Barr*

Page 278: *Karyn R. Millet*

Page 280: *Erik Kvalsvik*

Page 281: *Dominique Vorillon*

Page 282: *Tria Giovan*

Page 283: *Oberto Gili*

Page 284: *Jonn Coolidge*

Page 285: *Tim Beddow*

Page 286: *Erik Kvalsvik*

Page 288: *Edmund Barr*

Page 289: *Oberto Gili*

Page 290: *Karyn R. Millet*

Page 291: *Erik Kvalsvik*

Page 292: *Erik Kvalsvik*

Page 293: *J. Savage Gibson*

Page 294: *Eric Piasecki*

Page 295: *John Ellis*

Page 296: *Laura Moss*

Page 297: *Grey Crawford*

Page 298: *Roger Davies*

Page 299: *Ben Duggan*

Page 300: *Edmund Barr*

Page 301: *Oberto Gili*

Page 302: *J. Savage Gibson*

Page 303: *Grey Crawford*

Page 304: *Erik Kvalsvik*

Page 306: *Grey Crawford*

Page 307: *Tria Giovan*

Page 308: *Erik Kvalsvik*

Page 309: *Erik Kvalsvik*

Page 310: *Christopher Baker*

Page 311: *Tria Giovan*

Page 312: *Tria Giovan*

Page 313: *Tim Beddow*

Page 314: *Tria Giovan*

Page 315: *Oberto Gili*

Page 316: *Vincent Motte*

Page 317: *Nina Bramhall*

Page 318: *Tria Giovan*

Page 319: *Erik Kvalsvik*

Page 320: *Curtice Taylor*

Page 321: *John M. Hall*

Page 322: *Mick Hales*

Page 323: *Tim Street-Porter*

Page 324: *Nina Bramhall*

Page 325: *Vivian Russell*

Page 326: *Roger Davies*

Page 327: *Tim Beddow*

Page 328: *Karyn R. Millet*

Page 329: *Mick Hales*

Page 330: *Tim Street-Porter*

Index